LIFE DECODED
–The Science Way

Tapash Bose

PUSTAK MAHAL®

Publishers
Pustak Mahal®

Administrative office and sale centre
J-3/16 , Daryaganj, New Delhi-110002
☎ 23276539, 23272783, 23272784 • *Fax:* 011-23260518
E-mail: info@pustakmahal.com • *Website:* www.pustakmahal.com

Branches
Bengaluru: ☎ 080-22234025 • *Telefax:* 080-22240209
E-mail: pustak@airtelmail.in • pustak@sancharnet.in
Mumbai: ☎ 022-22010941, 022-22053387
E-mail: rapidex@bom5.vsnl.net.in
Patna: ☎ 0612-3294193 • *Telefax:* 0612-2302719
E-mail: rapidexptn@rediffmail.com

ISBN 978-81-223-1459-5

Edition: 2013

Printed at : **Radha Offset, Delhi**

Dedicated to

Jhuma

Contents

Acknowledgements

My humble *PRANAMs* to Lord Ganeshji for His kind blessings and inspiration and to Devi Saraswati for the power bestowed by Her to convert my disconnected thoughts and imagination into some meaningful text.

I convey my regards and gratitude to our great leader Sh. Girish Kumar (our present General Manager) who has been inspiring all of us to understand practical principles of management, leadership responsibilities, gaining satisfaction through meaningful contribution and the basic principles of value-based life. He has also inspired us go through and understand three life-changing books namely, *You Can Win* by Sh. Shib Kheda; *Seven Habits of Highly Effective People* by Stephen R Covey and *As a Man Thinketh* by James Allen. Many concepts of life are easily understood in these three great books. I am grateful to Prof. S.K.Chakraborty, retired renowned faculty from IIM, Kolkata and an authority in Value-based leadership & Ethical practices as I re-learnt many '*Bhartiya*' concepts and fundamentals which our society is tending to forget and shamelessly adopting even non-compatible western ways of living life.

I have also used the words of Swami Vivekananda at number of places as no other text is more appropriate at those contexts. Short stories/anecdotes have been taken from various mails received from friends and colleagues, Speaking tree of TOI, and the above-mentioned books. Some concepts have been adopted from *The Secret* by Rhonda Byrne.

I also thank all my seniors, peers, colleagues, team members in R&D and HR for giving me inputs on practical aspects of life through day-to-day formal and informal interactions (and chatting over lunch/ tea time).

I convey my heartiest thanks to the Pustak Mahal editorial team for selecting my material for publishing and special thanks to my Editor for patiently going through my raw draft and converting it to a presentable book. Last, but not the least, I must thank my son Gogol (Anjishnu), my daughter Titli (Anwesha) and my all time best friend & dear wife *Jhuma* for all the motivation & inspiration, giving the basic conceptual idea of comparing life with science, back-end support, clicking the right title, giving ideas about the cover, word-entry in PC, listening patiently to the draft so many times, for correcting & improving the concepts, anecdotes and for enhancing my language.

My sincere thanks to all the readers for patronising the book. Any feedback (positive or otherwise) will be my further source of inspiration.

Tapash Bose
tapashbosebel@gmail.com
My blog: www.sensiblemgmt.com

1. Introduction – Science in Life

Science is an endless ongoing quest to find logical answers to everything and an attempt to predict results with defined set of inputs in a given context, based on experiments, observations, analysis or calculations. It takes help of definitions, measuring units, formulae and laws to correlate them and observations for confirmation. Science always tries to find out what are the causes, what are the effects and what are the correlations between causes and effects and what is its pattern.

Science uses concepts like hypotheses, theory and laws to express the truths of physical world. All these terms are different though very similar. First, let us try to understand these terms in our context.

A hypothesis is an educated guess, based on observation. Usually, a hypothesis can be supported or refuted through experimentation or more observation. The funny thing is a hypothesis can be disproven, but not proven to be true.

For example, if you don't see any difference in the cleaning ability of various laundry detergents, you might hypothesize that cleaning effectiveness is not affected by the detergent you use. You can see this hypothesis can be disproven if a stain is removed by one particular detergent and not another. On the other hand, you cannot prove the hypothesis. Even if you never see a difference in the cleanliness of your clothes after trying a thousand detergents, there might be one you haven't tried that could be different.

The next level is theory. A scientific theory summarizes a hypothesis or group of hypotheses that have been supported with repeated testing. A theory is valid as long as there is no evidence to dispute it. Therefore, theories can be disproven. Basically, if evidence accumulates to support a hypothesis, then the hypothesis can become accepted as a good explanation of a phenomenon. So, one definition of a theory is to say it's an accepted hypothesis.

The next level is law, which generalizes a body of observations. At the time it is made, no exceptions have been found to a law. Scientific laws explain things, but they do not describe them. One way to tell a law and a theory apart is to ask if the description gives you a means to explain 'why'. A law is an analytic statement, usually with an empirically determined constant.

Science has given and will be giving numerous laws and theories (and hypotheses also) which deal with the issues and observations and logics of real physical world. That world is not limited to our tiny planet only, it expands to the whole universe or may be beyond that. That world is not limited in time scale to present and recent past only, but it expands to as early as the BIG beginning and gives projections for the times to come in its logical framework.

Now, we will try something funny. If we look at the laws and theories of science, we will find that for most of them there are conceptually exact or near equivalent and parallels available in our lives. Our life, actions and thoughts exist in the same physical world (which is governed by science) only, but has the additional complex dimensions of our brain, heart, mind, thoughts, emotions, relationships, motives, values, context and so many other things (both physical and non-physical). We will try to see how many of the laws of science are applicable to our lives and our behaviours & can be converted to hypotheses of life.

The laws and theories of science are structured as per chapters & sub-chapters of different branches of science namely Physics, Chemistry, Biology, Mathematics etc. Since, it is very difficult to structure the hypotheses of life in a sequence of chapters and sub-chapters of life as a whole; we shall try to follow the sequence of theories of science (where I will be more comfortable). In fact, considering the vastness of the domain of science, we have selected the branch 'Physics' only for this exercise.

Before going into the chapters of Physics, we will start with a very basic pillar of science which is the interlinkage of cause and effect.

Causality Principle

The principle states that cause must always precede effect. More formally, if an event *A* ("the cause") somehow influences an event *B* ("the effect") which occurs later in time, then event *B* cannot in turn have an influence on event *A*. That is, event *B* must occur at a later time *t* than event *A*, and further, all frames must agree upon this ordering.

This is a very fundamental principle of science as well as life. Everything happens because of some cause which triggers the effect. In some cases, we are the creators of those causes and in some other cases, we initiate the causes which gets further supplemented by some external linked forces. For example, if we take care of our health in terms of exercises and diet, there is high likelihood of staying healthy and if we do not do so, there is likelihood of having early health problems. If we do well in studies or in work, there is high likelihood of us getting duly rewarded. If we go to the railway station in time, we get the right train (normally). If we drive rash on road, there is high likelihood of meeting with an accident. If a sapling is born, there must have been seeds sown intentionally or unintentionally. If there is rain, there must be cloud behind that. If there is cloud, there must have been seas and oceans to provide water vapour and also the energy of sun to do so. On the other side, there may be again umpteen number of incidents which may not quite happen that way in spite of appropriately taking care of the right triggers. But, if we analyse them deeply, we will find that the other types of outcomes are for some other causes which we ignored or failed to take into consideration.

As per our ancient and evergreen philosophy, it's not the only birth we are having, we had many and will have many more. And all the effects in present life are due to the causes of our KARMA in this life as well as the lives lived earlier. Similarly, the effects of our KARMA in this life will be seen now and in future lives. There are threads of linkages which are clearly visible and tangible as well as invisible and intangible.

In fact, the nature's law of cause and effect can be converted to moral law of cause and effect with following postulates (taken from the book of Prof. S.K. Chakraborty):

- ☞ A cause at present must produce some effect in future.
- ☞ An effect at present must have had some cause in the past.
- ☞ The effect returns to the source of the cause.
- ☞ Each cause produces its own effect, there is no mutual cancellation.

Let us read a story to understand that things happen for a reason:

The brand new pastor and his wife, newly assigned to their first ministry, to reopen a church in suburban Brooklyn, arrived in early October excited about their opportunities. When they saw their church, it was very run down and needed much work. They set a goal to have everything done in time to have their first service on Christmas Eve.

They worked hard on repairing pews, plastering walls, painting, etc. and were just about to finish on December 18, which was much before the scheduled time. On December 19, a terrible tempest - a driving rainstorm hit the area and lasted for two days. On the 21st, the pastor went over to the church. His heart sank when he saw that the roof had leaked, causing a large area of plaster about 20 feet by 8 feet to fall off the front wall of the sanctuary just behind the pulpit, beginning about head high. The pastor cleaned up the mess on the floor, and not knowing what else to do but postpone the Christmas Eve service, headed home. On the way, he noticed that a local business was having a flea market type sale for charity, so he stopped in. One of the items was a beautiful, handmade, ivory coloured, crocheted tablecloth with exquisite work, fine colours and a cross embroidery right in the center. It was just the right size to cover the hole in the front wall. He bought it and headed back to the church.

By this time, it had started to snow. An older woman running from the opposite direction was trying to catch the bus. She missed it. The pastor invited her to wait in the warm church for the next bus scheduled 45 minutes later.

She sat in a pew and paid no attention to the pastor while he got a ladder, hangers, etc., to put up the tablecloth as a wall tapestry. The pastor could hardly believe how beautiful it looked and it covered up the entire problem area. Then he noticed the woman walking down the center aisle. Her face was white as a sheet. "Pastor," she asked, "where did you get that tablecloth from?" The pastor explained. Later, the woman asked him to check the lower right corner to see if the initials, EBG were crocheted into it there. They were. These were the initials of the woman, and she had made this tablecloth 35 years ago, in Austria. The woman could hardly believe it as the pastor told how he had just gotten "The Tablecloth".

The woman explained that before the war she and her husband were doing well people in Austria. When the Nazis came, she was forced to leave. Her husband was going to follow her the next week. He was captured, sent to prison and never saw her husband or her home again.

The pastor wanted to give her the tablecloth; but she made the pastor keep it for the church. The pastor insisted on driving her home. That was the least he could do. She lived on the other side of Staten Island and was only in Brooklyn for the day for a housecleaning job. What a wonderful service they had on Christmas Eve. The church was almost full. The music and the spirit were great. At the end of the service, the pastor and his wife greeted everyone at the door and many said that they would return. One older man, whom the pastor recognized from the neighbourhood continued to sit in one of the pews and stare, and the pastor wondered why he wasn't leaving.

The man asked him where he got the tablecloth on the front wall because it was identical to one that his wife had made years ago when they lived in Austria before the war and how could there be two tablecloths so much alike. He told the pastor how the Nazis came, how he forced his wife to flee for her safety and he was supposed to follow her, but he was arrested and put in a prison. He never saw his wife or his home again in all the 35 years between. The pastor asked him if he would allow him to take him for a little ride. They drove to Staten Island and to the same house where the pastor had taken the woman three days earlier. He helped the man climb the three flights of stairs to the woman's apartment, knocked on the door and he saw the greatest Christmas reunion he could ever imagine.

> ***Everything happens for a reason, we understand some, we do not understand some.***

(True Story-submitted by Pastor Rob Reid/Gautam Sanyal)

❑❑❑

2. Motion

This initial part of Physics deals with the concepts of rest and motion, distance and displacement, speed and velocity & acceleration. This is followed by the concept of inertia, force, momentum and the famous Newton's laws of motion. We will touch a few theories and concepts and try to get their real life equivalence.

Newton's First Law

We will come to these three famous laws, one by one, which brings in the concept of force. **Newton's first law states that every object will remain at its state of rest or of uniform motion until it is compelled to change it by the application of an external force.** This also gives the concept of inertia which is the property of an object to retain its state of rest or of uniform motion. Inertia depends on very basic feature of the object, which is its mass. More the mass, more is the inertia of an object.

The concept of **inertia of rest** is easily understood. Nothing moves on its own in this world. If it's an object, somebody has to push or pull to change its state from rest to motion. If it's a living being, it will move if it needs to do so. Otherwise, the state of rest on a comfortable chair (or sofa or bed) is the most stable state. But the inertia of motion is little complex in physical world. We do not find moving objects to move on endlessly with uniform speed. In fact, we find that unless an external force is applied, the moving objects tend to stop after some time. We know the reason, it is the friction – either of ground, or of water or of air.

We will tackle friction in second law. In the world of physics there are many practical examples of this first law. For example, if we are sitting in a bus and it suddenly starts, we tend to bend backward. Similar is the case when the bus suddenly stops we bend forward. Both these phenomena take place because of inertia. The lower part of our body, which is in touch with the seat and thus in turn with the bus, attain the state of inertia of motion in the first case as soon as the bus starts. But, the upper part of the body tries to retain the same state of inertia, i.e, inertia of rest and hence remains at its own previous position. This results in a conflict in the body, with lower part moving ahead and upper part staying behind. The opposite happens when the bus suddenly stops. So, the crux of the matter is anything tries to retain its state of rest or of uniform motion, wherever it is or in whichever state it is. One needs to pull or push to change that state of inertia.

In inertia of motion, there is something like inertia of direction also. Suppose a car is moving straight and there are some baggage tied onto its top. The car has to take a turn or bend suddenly. What happens to the baggage? There are high chances that the baggage will fly off unless tied very properly. This happens because the baggage had inertia of motion in a particular direction. As the car suddenly changed its direction, the baggage still tried to retain its original direction.

Now in human life, we see lot of equivalence to this first law. We derive the following:

☞ Every individual has some amount of inertia for doing a task, which is a kind of laziness or lethargy exhibited by the individual. The inertia here does not depend on physical mass of the individual directly (other than the interpretation that normally the heavier people find it difficult to move compared to others), but it depends on some inner capability and tendency – which is the mental mass.

- ☞ Inertia of human being also depends on the nature of task. A highly ambitious person will have very low hurdle of inertia in his professional front and will swiftly take a start in his race for success. A happy-go-lucky kind of person will show high inertia for professional initiatives and will find multiple number of excuses to avoid the task, but may show relatively low inertia and high enthusiasm to go for a party. In home-front, some men love to go for shopping with wives but some find it very difficult to overcome the weekend inertia.

- ☞ One has to do lot of pushing or pulling to change the state of rest (i.e, the state of no progress or growth) to that of motion (which signifies progress and growth). So the simple secret of progress is appropriate hard-work – physical or mental or both.

- ☞ In our journey of life, we should not put the accelerator or brake suddenly. This may cause conflict amongst different parts of our personality and mental state caused by jerk in the movement. Also, we should not change our direction of life suddenly. Then the knowledge and skill acquired may suddenly become redundant. The change in direction should be tried out gently and smoothly.

☞ So, the law of inertia is applicable to human beings in a little complex manner. We tend to remain at the state of rest unless compelled by a force to change to state of motion. Here the difference is that this force need not be external only, it can be internal also (in fact, it is more effective when the drive is internal). It's not that effective if you are always driven by your parents, elders, teachers and bosses to perform and perform well; it is always more effective if someone inside you drives you. So, we can move in life not under compulsion, but by our inner urge to do so, which is called passion. And, in most cases, motion in right direction is life. And, to achieve motion, force is a must. Hence, there is no substitute for hard work.

Let us read a story from nature to understand the importance of motion:

A tale of two seas

The Dead Sea is really a lake, not a sea. It is so high in salt content that the human body can float easily. One can almost lie down and read a book!

The salt in the Dead Sea is as high as 35% - almost 10 times that of normal ocean water. And all that saltiness has meant that there is no life at all in the Dead Sea. No fish. No vegetation. No sea animals. No marine life of any sort. Nothing lives in the Dead Sea. Hence the name: DEAD SEA.

It turns out that there is Sea of Galilee is just north of the Dead Sea. Both, the Sea of Galilee and the Dead Sea, receive their water from river Jordan. Yet, they are very, very different. Unlike the Dead Sea, the Sea of Galilee is pretty, resplendent with rich, colourful marine life. There are lots of plants and lot of fish, too. In fact, the sea of Galilee is home to over twenty different types of fish. Same region, same source of water, and yet, one sea is full of life, the other is dead. How come?

Here is the answer.

The River Jordan flows into the Sea of Galilee and then flows out. The water simply passes through the Sea of Galilee in and out and that keeps the Sea healthy and vibrant, teeming with marine life. But, the Dead Sea is so far below the sea level, that it has no outlet. The water flows in from the river Jordan, but does not flow out. There are no outlet streams at all. It is estimated that over a million tons of water evaporates from the Dead Sea every day, leaving it salty. It is too full of minerals and unfit for any marine life. The Dead Sea takes in water from the River Jordan, and holds it. It does not give/flow out. Result? No life at all.

If you remain static in the inertia of rest, you are dead; if you mix motion judiciously, you live and prosper.

Newton's Second Law

The second law states that the rate of change of momentum of an object is directly proportional to the external force applied on it and it takes place in the direction of applied force.

Second law gives rise to the concept of momentum which is the product of mass and velocity. It relates the rate of change of momentum to the applied force and it is finally derived from this law that, Force = Mass x Acceleration. So, this law gives the magnitude and direction of force.

There is another way to look at it in conjunction with first law. These are valid in true sense in ideal condition where there is no opposing force of friction. Otherwise, the initial part and some amount (may be small, may be significant) of the applied force will be exhausted in overcoming the friction force. Only after that the balance force is utilised in increasing the momentum. Many a times, the friction force is so high (or the force is so low) that in spite of applying force, no movement takes place.

☞ In life also, force is required to gain momentum. And the quantum of change of momentum depends on the force applied (be it external or internal) in terms of initiative taken, practice done, homework done, planning made.

- Moreover, like in Physics, the conditions are not ideal. To move ahead, to gain momentum, simply applying force is not sufficient. We must know and gauge the hurdles of friction in the path and apply force more and more to overcome those hurdles and move forward to gain momentum. If we fail once or twice or even more times, we should not give up and keep trying with more and more vigour. At some point of time, for some value of effort, the opposing friction will give up and things will start moving. If the effort is further increased, the rate of movement of progress will also increase proportionally.
- The first law implies that to progress in life, hardwork is must. The second law gives a measure of that hardwork which depends on both the progress targeted and the anticipated hurdles in terms of friction.
- The second law also exhibits the importance of perseverance. If the friction force is high, then the initial effort of push is not sufficient to move an object or make the progress initiated in life. Like, if we join a new school or new college or new organization (in general, a new set-up), we seem to be lost as our efforts apparently do not produce any movement. So, we

have to try again and again, put effort, put more effort and then we see little bit of positive progress. Here, perseverance is the key. And as the kinetic friction is less than static friction, once the initial hurdle is crossed, the effort required to sustain the motion in the same conditions becomes reduced in magnitude.

Don't wait for a light to appear at the end of the tunnel, stride down there and light the bloody thing yourself.

- Sara Henderson

Let us share some life examples:

Stories of winners

In 1962, four nervous young musicians played their first record audition for the executives of the Decca Recording Company. The executives were not impressed. While turning down this group of musicians, one executive said, "We don't like their sound. Groups of guitars are on the way out." **The group was called The Beatles.**

In 1944, Emmeline Snively, director of the Blue Book Modelling Agency told modelling hopeful Norma Jean Baker, "You'd better learn secretarial work or else get married." **She went on and became Marilyn Monroe.**

In 1954, Jimmy Denny, manager of the Grand Ole Opry, fired a singer after one performance.

He told him, "You ain't goin' nowhere....son. You ought to go back to drivin' a truck." ***He went on to become Elvis Presley.***

When **Alexander Graham Bell** *invented the telephone in 1876, it did not ring off the hook with calls from potential backers. After making a demonstration call, President Rutherford Hayes said, "That's an amazing invention, but who would ever want to see one of them?"*

When **Thomas Edison** *invented the light bulb, he tried over 2000 experiments before he got it to work. A young reporter asked him how it felt to fail so many times. He said, "I never failed once. I invented the light bulb. It just happened to be a 2000-step process."*

In the 1940s, another young inventor named Chester Carlson took his idea to 20 corporations, including some of the biggest in the country. They all turned him down. In 1947, after 7 long years of rejections, he finally got a tiny company in Rochester, NY, the Haloid Company, to purchase the rights to his invention -- an electrostatic paper-copying process. ***Haloid became Xerox Corporation.***

A little girl - the 20th of 22 children, was born prematurely and her survival was doubtful. When she was 4 years old, she contracted double pneumonia and scarlet fever, which left her with a paralysed left leg. At age 9, she removed the metal leg brace she had been dependent on and began to walk without it. By 13 she had developed a rhythmic walk, which doctors said was a miracle. That same year she decided to become a runner. She entered a race and came in last. For the next few years every race she entered, she came in last. Everyone told her to quit, but she kept on running. One day she actually won a race; and then another. From then on she won every race she entered. Eventually this little girl – ***Wilma Rudolph****, went on to win three Olympic gold medals.*

A school teacher scolded a boy for not paying attention to his mathematics and for not being able to solve simple problems. She told him that you would not become anybody in life. The boy was ***Albert Einstein.***

This was a man who failed in business at the age of 21;

Was defeated in a legislative race at age 22;

Failed again in business at age 24;

Overcame the death of his sweetheart at age 26;

Had a nervous breakdown at age 27;

Lost a congressional race at age 34;

Lost a senatorial race at age 45;

Failed in an effort to become vice-president at age 47;

Lost a senatorial race at age 49;

And he was elected president of the United States at age 52.

This man was **Abraham Lincoln**.

Every success story is also a story of great failure/s. To overcome friction and to gain momentum, quite an effort is required along with the mental will.

> ***A winner is NOT one who NEVER FAILS, but one who NEVER QUITS!***

Newton's Third Law

Newton's third law of motion states that to every action, there is an equal and opposite reaction.

This law has the simplest statement out of the three laws of motion but is the trickiest one. Hence, this requires a little bit of elaboration. Action and reaction are basically forces. Action is the force which takes place first from object A to object B. Reaction is the force which happens next (but at the same time) from object B to object A. So, they occur simultaneously and they act on different bodies so that the effect is not neutralized.

- ☞ In life, normally we get back from anyone the reaction in terms of behaviour which is commensurate to our action (i.e, our behaviour). It is said that 'Life is an echo'. It tends to happen immediately or over a larger domain of time span. If you are generally helpful to your friends, colleagues, relatives, unknown co-passengers, you tend to get help from them or even other unknown people when you require the same. On the other hand, if you are selfish and do not bother for others, then others normally do not bother for you. If you smile at others, others also smile at you; if you frown, you usually get back frowns only.

- But the problem with some people is that they do not recognize the existence of this law in life, though it is very much visible in nature. If we sow paddy, we get rice; if we sow wheat, we get wheat. Nature never mixes them up. But, unfortunately, some of the lesser mortals think that that even if they are crooked, rude & they exploit people or situations and make apparent progress, nothing wrong will happen to them. If we look closely at them, we will find the utter distress they are in, in their close personal front and the amount of stress and physical trouble they are going through. The credit and debit get balanced in one's cycle of life/lives and it all becomes a big zero at the end of it.

- Life sometimes goes a step further – it ensures reaction and it also ensures that it gets multiplied (this is not feasible in Physics). In any relationship, if you invest time, concern, trust, communication and so on, you normally get back more in turn though you do not expect (actually the return multiply only when you give unilaterally, without asking for or expecting anything in return). On the other hand, if you do not invest anything positive, you get back negatives only, and that too manifold.

☞ Action does not act in anticipation of reaction, but reaction happens on its own. Similarly, in nature, there is only law of giving, there is no natural law of taking. Taking happens automatically, giving has to be done. The tree gives its shadow, oxygen, flowers, fruits and in the end, wood to us asking nothing in return. The sun gives its infinite source of energy for life, the rivers give us water, the night gives us calmness, the moon gives us poetry, the rains give us water for farming and music at heart,……and so on.

☞ "*We are all traders in life, traders in virtues, traders in religion. And alas! we are also traders in love. Trading is give and take, buying and selling. We get caught not by what we give but by what we expect. We get misery in return for our love; not from the fact that we love, but from the fact that we want love in return. Desires must bring misery. Ask nothing; want nothing in return – be a perfectly unselfish man. Give what you have to give;*

it will come back to you – but do not think of it now. It will come back multiplied a thousand-fold – but the attention must not be on that. The more you give, the more it will come to you. The quicker you can empty the air out of the room, the quicker it will be filled up by the fresh external air." Swami Vivekananda.

We make a living by what we get, but we make a life by what we give.

- Winston Churchill

Let's read a story in this subject:

A glass of milk

One day, a poor boy, who was selling goods from door to door to pay his way through school, found he had only one thin dime left, and he was hungry. He decided he would ask for a meal at the next house. However, he lost his nerve when a lovely young woman opened the door. Instead of a meal he asked for a drink of water. However, she thought he looked hungry and so brought him a large glass of milk.

He drank it slowly, and then asked, 'How much do I owe you?'

'You don't owe me anything,' she replied. 'Mother has taught us never to accept pay for a kindness.'

He said, 'Then I thank you from my heart.'

As Howard Kelly left that house, he not only felt stronger physically, but his faith in God and man was also strong.

Years' later that young woman became critically ill. The local doctors were baffled. They finally sent her to a big city, where they called specialists to study her rare disease. Dr. Howard Kelly was called in for consultation. When he heard the name of the town she came from, a strange light filled his eyes. Immediately, he rose and went down the hall of the hospital to her room. Dressed in his doctor's gown he went in to see her. He recognised her at once.

He went back to her consultation room determined to do the best to save her life. From that day he gave special attention to the case. After a long struggle, the battle was won. Dr. Kelly requested the business office to pass the final bill to him for approval. He looked at it, and then wrote something on the edge and the bill was sent to her room. She feared to open it, for she was sure it would take the rest of her life to pay for it all. Finally she looked, and something caught her attention on the side of the bill. She read these words.... 'Paid in full with one glass of milk.'

Mother nature ensured that she gets back her genuine kindness in kind.

There can be another one in little lighter tone:

Fateful accident

A woman and a man were involved in a car accident. It was a bad one. Both their cars were totally smashed, but amazingly neither of them was hurt. After they crawled out of their cars, the woman said, 'So you're a man, that's interesting! I'm a woman. Wow, just look at our cars! There is nothing left, but fortunately we are unhurt. This must be a sign from God that we should meet and be friends and live together in peace for the rest of our days'.

The man replied, 'I agree with you completely. This must be a sign from God!'

The woman continued, 'And look at this: here's another miracle. My car is completely demolished, but this bottle of wine didn't break! Sure, God wants us to drink this wine and celebrate our good fortune'.

Then she handed the bottle to the man. The man nodded his head in agreement, opened it and drank half the bottle, and then handed it back to the woman. The woman took the bottle, immediately put the cap back on, and handed it back to the man. The man asked, 'Aren't you having any?'

The woman replied, 'No, I think I'll just wait for the police'.

Here reaction was little more than action.

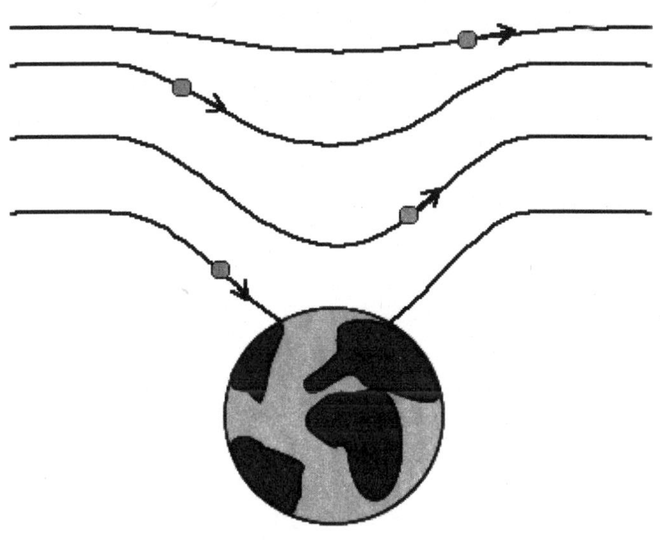

3. Gravitation

This part of Physics deals with the concepts of gravitation, gravity, weight, Kepler's laws of planetary motion etc.

Law of Gravitation

Every point mass attracts every single other point mass by a force pointing along the line intersecting both points. The force is proportional to the product of the two masses and inverserly proportional to the square of the distance between them

$$F = G\frac{m_1 m_2}{r^2}$$

G is universal gravitational constant.

It means that between two objects of given distance, the force of attraction will depend on the individual masses. This is called Universal Gravitational Law or Newton's Law of Gravitation.

This also implies that the force on both the objects m_1 and m_2 will be same. So the object with lighter mass will have more acceleration and the object with heavier mass will have less acceleration (as acceleration = force/mass). In special cases, when one mass is substantially heavier than the other and the objects are very near, then the smaller object falls on the heavier object, which remains stationary (as the apple falls on earth though the attraction force is same for both of them). And, if the objects are far away, then the lighter object may derive the centripetal force from this gravitational pull and keep happily rotating around the heavier object (like the moon rotating around earth, earth rotating around sun and so on). Same is the situation in real practical life we live in.

- ☞ If the objects are converted to human beings, the law can be read like this: 'between two human beings at a given distance of relationship, the effectiveness of the relationship will depend on product of individual commitment in that relationship'.
- ☞ More the commitment (like the mass), more fruitful is the output from the relationship. The commitment comes from mutual trust, mutual understanding and mutual investment in the relationship. "*Seek first to understand, before being understood*" – this is the fifth habit of

the "Seven habits of highly effective people" by *Stephen Covey*. First listen to understand, not just to frame a quick reply. Do not filter it or fit it in your own paradigm, own autobiography, try to place yourself in the other person's perspective. Then explain your position so that he/she understands you.

- ☞ More the distance between the hearts, less is the bondage of relationship (inversely proportional to the square). The distance reduces by enhanced communication and the capacity of giving.
- ☞ Gravitation is actually law of attraction in science which has its root in the natural law of attraction. The natural law of attraction states that we attract what we believe in our heart, not what we superficially want and we get the same. If we have a firm belief that we will succeed, we automatically put more and more effort and success comes to us. If we believe that we cannot do it, we do not do anything and we finally cannot do it. "*The soul attracts that which it secretly harbors, that which it loves, and also that which it fears. It reaches the height of its cherished aspirations. It falls to the level of its unchastened desires - and circumstances are the means by which*

the soul receives its own"- from As a Man Thinketh by James Allen.

☞ There is another kind of law of attraction. This is much easier to understand. We all have friends in school, college, university, professional life. We meet people in train-journey, air journey, meetings, parties. We have relatives and neighbours. But we have a preferred select group of people from all these lots with whom we are very comfortable, very close, and we feel involved in the interaction and there are others with whom we are not that comfortable. Why does this happen? This happens because we have some particular frequency of personality and we attract the persons with similar frequency and this happens naturally, unconsciously.

☞ *To smile without condition,*
To walk without intention,
To give without reason, &
To care without expectation,
Are the beauties of any Relation!

☞ For the extended interpretation, a great leader always has number of followers who either rotate around him or get totally submerged into him. Look at the lives of Gandhiji, Netaji, Pandit Nehru ji, Lal Bahadur Shastri ji, Sardar Patel, Dr. Abdul Kalam, Bill Gates, Ratan Tata and so on. They take along the whole organization or the whole society along with them for a vision, for a purpose, for a cause and for a zeal. Unfortunately, this is true for great dictators also (like Hitler, Mussolini, Stalin, Saddam Hussain etc. who also could muster voluminous following by using negative means). The only difference is that for dictator, the force is situational and fragile; while for true leader of character and achievements, this bondage is permanent and it even becomes stronger with time.

Let us read a story regarding this:

The story of penicillin

His name was Fleming, and he was a poor Scottish farmer. One day, while trying to make a living for his family, he heard a cry for help coming from a nearby bog. He dropped his tools and ran to the bog.

There, mired to his waist in black muck, was a terrified boy, screaming and struggling to free himself. Farmer Fleming saved the lad from what could have been a slow and terrifying death.

The next day, a fancy carriage pulled up to the Scotsman's sparse surroundings. An elegantly dressed nobleman stepped out and introduced himself as the father of the boy Farmer Fleming had saved. 'I want to repay you,' said the nobleman. 'You saved my son's life.'

'No, I can't accept payment for what I did,' the Scottish farmer replied waving off the offer. At that moment, the farmer's own son came to the door of the family hovel. 'Is that your son?' the nobleman asked.

'Yes,' the farmer replied proudly. The nobleman said, 'I'll make you a deal. Let me provide him with the level of education my own son will enjoy. If the lad is anything like his father, he'll no doubt grow to be a man we both will be proud of.'

And that he did

Farmer Fleming's son attended the very best schools and in time, graduated from St. Mary's Hospital Medical School in London, and went on to become known throughout the world as the noted Sir Alexander Fleming, the discoverer of Penicillin.

Years afterward, the same nobleman's son who was saved from the bog was stricken with pneumonia. What saved his life this time? Penicillin. The name of the nobleman? Lord Randolph Churchill. His son's name? Sir Winston Churchill.

The commitments shown by the two individuals resulted not only in their fruitful relationship, but also great boon to the human society as a whole.

Gravity & Law of Escape Velocity

Gravity is the special name given to the gravitational force of attraction by earth on the objects on and around it. Every object on or around earth (within reasonable range) are attracted by it towards its centre by this force of gravity (which is actually governed by Universal Gravitational Law, already discussed). So, whenever normally something moves upwards, its velocity goes on decreasing and it reaches zero & then finally starts coming back towards the ground. Exceptions are the rockets which move into space breaking the barrier of gravity. How do they do that? Here comes the concept of Escape velocity. **Escape velocity is the speed at which the kinetic energy plus the gravitational potential energy of an object is zero. Simply speaking, it is the speed needed to "break free" from a gravitational field without further propulsion**.

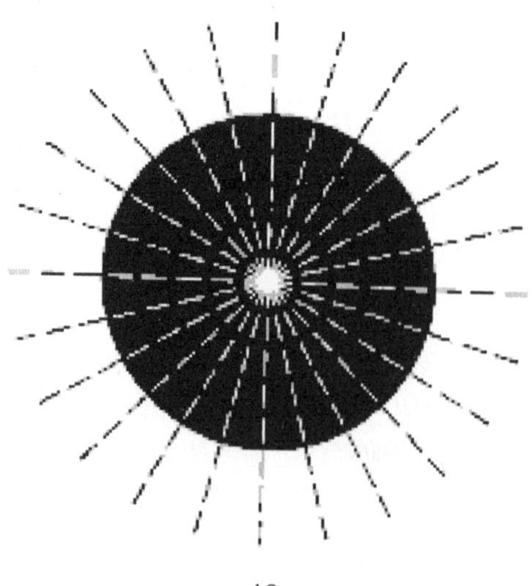

For a spherically-symmetric body, escape velocity is calculated by the formula

$$v_e = \sqrt{\frac{2GM}{r}}$$

where G is the universal gravitational constant ($G = 6.67 \times 10^{-11}$ m^3 kg^{-1} s^{-2}), M the mass of the planet (here, earth) or other heavenly body, and r the distance from the centre of gravity.

☞ In real life, we are not concerned about the formula, but the concept is important. In all kinds of situations, we and our movements & thoughts are continuously controlled by the core of the situation which is similar to core of gravitational attraction of earth. Many a times, we feel that we shall be able to overcome the effect of the situation by gaining sufficient velocity. Sometimes, we are correct in gauging ourselves and most of the times we are wrong. So many a times, we remain entangled within the field of gravity and start falling back towards the centre after reaching certain height.

☞ In relationship conflicts and arguments, logics and counter-logics do not help diffusing the situation at all. Frayed tempers, frowning eyebrows, sentimental outbursts further bring the parties to the core of the issue only. The way to come out of it is rational thinking, mutual compromise based on understanding and trust. Otherwise, we will keep on nose-diving back to the zero level.

- ☞ The habit 6 of Seven habits of highly effective people is 'Synergise'. It means that the whole is greater than the sum of individual parts if they are added in an appropriate manner. We have to open ourselves up, understand the genuine problems of each other, understand to the practical extent we can go without becoming losers, look for the good in others, have trust in others, think beyond personal shell of 'me', look for alternatives, look for solutions. Then only we can accumulate energy to come out of the core of the problem and reach the sky of solution through escape velocity.

- ☞ The pull by the earth's gravity can also be compared with our comfort zone. We all build our comfort zone in our professional and personal life and we are very comfortable out there. But that leads to a very ordinary kind of life – there is no progress and no thrill in that. If we want to really flourish in life, we have to look for changes and innovations. We have to take calculated risks. We have to continually increase our competencies, make our performance better and better, contribute more than we get, accept challenges beyond our roles – only then we can be visible to the world, only then we can rise above the ordinary, only then we can escape from the gravity and move skywards.

☞ If the problem at hand is ordinary, normally the solution is also ordinary. If the challenge itself is orbit-shifting, then there is no ordinary solution. We have to individually and collectively achieve innovation by out-of-the-box thinking to get a solution and convert the challenge into opportunity. If we look at the formula, we see that it has two constants 2 and G in the formula for which we cannot do anything. There are two variables – M and r – the mass and the radius of the planet, which are the inherent parameters of the problem itself. So, once the problem or the issue is identified with its known complexity and volume (M and r), the value of escape velocity gets pre-defined. There is no short-cut now. It's then only the game of how to do it – what rocket is to be used (what resources), which fuel (which team), which launcher (which process or technique – existing or new) and all that.

We must be skilful enough to gauge the escape velocity required and act accordingly.

Let's read a story of our college days in a lighter tone regarding situational escape velocity:

Story of mess strike

It was another exam time, the end-sem of fourth year, which was to start the next day. The rumours became strong that there may be a mess strike. But, many of us were not paying much attention to it as such rumours have come during last exams also and we wasted time in rejoicing which finally proved to be very expensive as the strike never materialized.

I got up little late for the exam day and heard little hulla-gulla downstairs. It was a kind of festive atmosphere downstairs with everyone hugging each other. Nihar and Debsha came running towards me, "Mess strike boss, indefinite mess strike........."

I entered the mess after about half an hour. There were whole lot of others also. The planning was going on for how to face this sudden crisis of arranging some makeshift breakfast and may be lunch also. As usual, in such a big crowd of geniuses, and that too, containing so many "expert" cooks, it was becoming very difficult to draw a concrete action plan and actually doing some ground work. Finally, some of them realized this and started looking for some vessel for making coffee.

So, the activities started. We put one big degchi of milk for boiling. Sugar was added generously as stock was no issue. Only handling the huge vessel was getting a little tricky. Along with coffee, bread-toast was to be served. In such mass-scale, breads are toasted on inverted karai, which is heated on some burner. Again, this is much trickier compared to toasting bread at home where the heating rate is much slower. Here, we were placing dozens of bread together on the karai, which initially takes some time in getting heated. But, once heated, it transfers the heat very fast to the breads and if one is little lacking in concentration, the breads will simply get black. In spite of lots of coordinating activities, the output was coming to around 75% only.

But, nobody minded that and everyone enjoyed the breakfast of bread, butter and coffee. Immediately after breakfast, we had to indulge in planning and action for lunch, which was a relatively tougher job. The experts ruled out chapattis in the very beginning and there was no dispute on that.

"Won't it be fun if we make khichdi instead? We can add up spicy papad with that along with mixed veg." commented Nihar.

"Not a bad idea", Prithwis said "but we should take the non-bongs' opinion also as this is a typical Bengali dish".

On crisis situations, the whole nation gets united on single agenda – why not Azad hall? There were no issues with anyone, khichdi or any damn food. So, there was smoking khichdi, fried papad and mixed veg served for lunch around 1:00 pm. Needless to say, all and all enjoyed every bit of it.

When post-lunch winding up was going on, flash news came (the term of 'breaking news' was not there those days) that the talks between IIT authorities and Mess workers has failed and the strike will continue. There was a scene of jubilation all around in anticipation of holidays. The news spread like fire and by 5:00 pm almost 90% of the students had finished 90% packing to move out after the formal declaration from the authorities. The koels of joy were singing all around "koo, koo, ...", how sweet!

So, we all decided that we'd have a lavish experimental dinner (kind of break-up dinner before long vacation). This time Anis, Hebbar, Rob, Jayaram, Kochu (Amarnath) volunteered to organize vegetable fried rice with scrambled eggs served separately. Some more volunteers joined in to help them cut small pieces of carrots, beans, capsicum, onion, peas etc. The smell of ghee, kaju and the flavoured rice spread all around and added flavour to the festive mood. The music system in the common room was playing the evergreen songs of Beatles to the full volume fully supported by the 'koels of joy' kooing sweetly all around in our mental horizon. The formal declaration from the institute was to come any moment.

I think we crossed all limits of enjoying the joy and same must have been the scenario in other halls also. In such kind of scenario, the process inches towards the anticipated climax and almost attains it, but the small gap between almost attaining and actually attaining is not fulfilled as the system fails to achieve the required escape velocity. The climax gets itself converted to anti-climax and the flying object nosedives back to ground by the action of gravity.

In simpler words, just when Anis was adding the last bunches of green peas in the karai, somebody from nowhere appeared and announced to the utter shock and disbelief of everyone, "Mess strike has been called off. They are joining duties right now."

It was like a bombshell to all. We didn't know whether to blame the mess workers or the IIT authorities for coming to an agreement in the late evening. The koels of joy nosedived and the crows of sorrow and despair started screaming all over "ka, ka, ka,…."

> ***Oh, forgot to mention the final component of the anti-climax of nosedive - the exams were to resume the next day as per the balanced schedule!***

❑❑❑

4. Work and Energy

This part of Physics deals with thrust & pressure, buoyant force, Archimedes' principle, flow of fluid. This also deals with work, power and energy.

Archimedes' Principle

There is an interesting story of this discovery of this famous law where we will not go into (Eureka and all that). This principle is about the change of apparent weight of a solid object when immersed in a fluid. **It states that when an object is fully or partially immersed in a fluid, it experiences an upward buoyant force. This buoyant force is equal to the weight of the displaced fluid.**

The buoyant force always acts upwards and hence the apparent weight of the object gets reduced compared to its actual weight in air. The extent of this reduction depends on the volume of fluid displaced (and hence the volume of the object) and the density of the fluid. As a result, the object feels lighter and if the buoyant force equals the actual weight of the object, the object starts floating on the fluid. That is why we feel lighter inside water.

The key here is the volume of the object for the given mass, which is under our control. If we increase the volume for same mass, the buoyant force will be more and even the sinking kind of objects can float. That is how a ship, made of iron, floats in water whereas an iron rod simply sinks.

☞ Similarly, in life, we do not have much option about the fluid, which is the surrounding where we live and work.

We do not have much control about the weight - which is the sum total of issues, problems, burdens of life at different times. The only way to reduce those burdens and remain happy is increasing our volume of hope and positive thoughts (and, of course, work for those issues to reduce the actual weight ultimately).

- ☞ There is another angle in life which is 'one must not make rules for how everyone else should behave'. Then, when the world does not obey your rules, you get angry. You may have simple expectations like:
- ☞ Friends should return favours.
- ☞ People should appreciate you.
- ☞ Planes and trains should arrive in time.
- ☞ Everyone should be honest.
- ☞ Your spouse or best friend should remember your birthday.

These expectations may sound reasonable and simple (like floating of a reasonably heavy object in water). But often, these things won't happen. So you end up frustrated and disappointed (sinking in the fluid), though there may be genuine reasons for not getting that expected response. So, there is a better strategy: demand less, and instead, have preferences!

For things that are beyond your control, tell yourself: 'I would prefer this, but if it happens otherwise, it's OK too' [expand your volume to remain floating using the benefit of buoyant force]. You prefer that people are polite. But, even when few persons are rude, it does not ruin your day. You prefer sunshine... but if it rains, it is OK too.

☞ In the first habit of Seven habits of highly effective people, the great author *Stephen Covey* has given the concepts of two circles which we make in our mental frame – the circle of influence and the circle of concern. The circle of influence consists of those parameters in life on which we have direct control – like what I eat, how much I take care of my health, how much I study, how much time I give to my family, how proactive I am at work, how much I save etc etc. So, I have direct access and control on all these things and so their good or bad is my direct responsibility. The circle of influence contributes to the volume of my vessel of life. Hence my efforts should be concentrated in expanding its volume as much as possible so that I get a good buoyant force which helps me to float easily, happily, comfortably, successfully in the water of life. On the other side, the circle of concern contains things for which we do not have any direct control – like, the weather, the economic policies, the stock market, the recession, terrorism, past regrets, coworkers' gossips etc. The circle of concern just contributes to the weight of my vessel of life. So, our effort should be to make it as small as possible by being just aware of them and live with them using circle of influence but not feeling helpless about them so that the weight of the vessel of life does not increase unnecessarily.

Let's read a small activity:

Raising a glass of water

A lecturer was giving a lecture to his student on stress management.

He raised a glass of water and asked the audience, "How heavy do you think this glass of water is?"

The students' answers ranged from 200 to 500 gm.

'Can you hold this simple thing for a minute?' he asked. 'Yes' was the combined answer from all.

'What about an hour?' he asked.

The students looked at each other and one of them said, 'we can hold but it may cause pain to our hand.'

'You're right. If you hold it for a day, you will have to call an ambulance. Isn't it funny? It is the exact same weight, but the longer you hold it, the heavier it becomes', he said.

The students agreed.

"It does not matter on the absolute weight. It depends on how long you hold it. If we carry burdens all the time, sooner or later, we will not be able to carry on, the burden becoming increasingly heavier", the teacher explained. There was agreement in audience.

"What you have to do is to put the glass down, rest for a while before holding it up again. We have to put down the burden periodically, so that we can be refreshed and are able to carry on" he further explained.

'So, before you return home from work tonight, put the burden of work down. Don't carry it back home. You can pick it up tomorrow' he concluded.

Whatever burdens you are having now on your shoulders, let it down for a moment if you can. Pick it up again later when you have rested..............

Rest and relax, expand your volume and increase the buoyant force.

Life is short, enjoy it!!

> ***Dream as if you'll live forever. Live as if you'll die today.***
>
> ***- James Dean***

In the end what matters most is, how well did you live, love, and learn to let go.

Equation of Continuity

This is regarding flow of fluid through a pipe. **This states that a fluid flowing through a pipe flows at a rate which is inversely proportional to the cross-sectional area of the pipe**. That is, if the pipe constricts, the fluid flows faster; if it widens, the fluid flows slower. It is in essence a restatement of the conservation of mass during constant flow.

Mathematically it can be expressed as $v_1 * A_1 = v_2 * A_2$, where v and A represent the velocity and cross-sectional areas at two points.

- ☞ In our life, we have umpteen numbers of relationships since our birth and we undergo n-times that number of relationship-episodes in our life. Many of the incidents are normal and ordinary, while few are extra-ordinary and landmark events. But, even for landmark events for you with someone else, it is not necessary that it will be equally landmark for the other person as it is to you. For example, you might have been helped by your old school teacher to take a vital decision regarding your branch of studies and you are thankful to him for the entire lifetime. But, if you go and ask that teacher about that incident, it might be an ordinary event for him as he has been doing it for many students over ages. So, as area (A) increases, the flow-rate (v) decreases and the product remains constant. We must always be conscious and sensitive to the context and perspective of any relationship episode between two individuals and appreciate that same episode (same fluid flowing) may have different impacts (flow-rates) to different individuals depending on the perspective (area of pipe).

☞ To make it little more precise, every relationship episode in life between you and your counterpart (which may be varying) has two perceptions – one by you and one by the other party. The importance or significance of the episode will be different to both of you which will depend on the relative level of importance of the relationship and the product will be constant. It means, the person at lower level in relationship, will assign a higher order of significance to the episode. Not only that, his (the person at lower level) expectation will also be higher. Taking the same example of the school teacher, who is at higher level of relationship w.r.t the student, will consider the episode as a routine one. On the other side, for the student, it is a landmark event.

☞ Since the expectation levels are different in a relationship (based on mutual relationship level), the person at the higher orbit must appreciate and acknowledge the feelings and expectations of the other person. This showing of empathy does not cost anything other than devoting some time for listening, showing concern etc; but this goes a long way in relationship building and even loyalty building.

Let's go through an anecdote experienced by my colleague in this regard:

The call at midnight

The mobile rang at very odd hour in the night. I could not make out what the time was. 'Who's it?' Rajesh asked me in half-sleep.

It was a number displayed, no name was there. So, it's not from my known contacts. Should I take the call or not, I thought. Parallelly, I just recalled my friend telling me last week about a call at 2:00 am which raised her heartbeat which turned out to be a recorded commercial call. She subsequently complained to the service provider, but of no result. In these thoughts and in this process of dilemma, the call ended. I went back to sleeping posture.

It might have been just a few minutes, when the mobile rang in a different tune. This time this was Rajesh's. He jumped up and said, 'It's the same number, I have to talk to the idiot'.

'Who's there?' he screamed.

'Sir, is madam ji there?' was the response. So, it was not a recorded commercial call.

'Who are you calling at this time?' Rajesh asked.

'Sir, I am security staff of the office. I am to tell madam something', he said.

Rajesh handed over the mobile to me and said, 'It's some security fellow of your office, now you handle.'

'What happened?' I asked.

'Madam ji, I am Madan Singh reporting from main gate. One thief was trying to steal and we have caught him, madam', he said.

'Very good, then keep him at your custody. Have you reported to Security officer?' I said in sleepy tone.

'Yes mam ji, he only told me to report to you also.'

'Ok Madan ji, what has he told you to do with him?' I asked.

'He told me to hand over to police thana in the morning.'

'Do that and now you need not inform me anything more', I said and we went back to sleep.

I reached office in time in the morning and almost forgot the late night incident. But I got reminded of the case seeing the security guard at the gate. That Madan Singh saluted me little extra at the entry and reached my cabin within fifteen minutes. 'Madamji, good morning', he saluted again.

'Good morning', I said, taking my eyes of the bunch of files on my table (and side rack).

'Madam ji, that thief ......' he continued.

'Yes, what happened to that thief?' I asked, though

I was not really in a mood to go into the detail. But as a responsible HR head, I needed to know the end of the story. Moreover, he has done his job well.

'We took him to Thana Link road at the same time', he explained.

'Then?' I asked.

'They told us to come after 6:00 am as the incharge for such cases was not there.'

'Then?' I repeated.

'We had to take care of that fellow till 6:00 am and then we went there again', he continued.

'So, now he is at their charge?' I asked.

'No, madam ji, the thanawala said that such theft does not come under their jurisdiction and we should report to the local police chowki only.'

'Oh, you had to do lot of running around Madan ji', I expressed my sympathies.

'Yes, madam ji. At last we could put that thief in the hands of the police chowki. That too, one of the constables was known to me as he is from a neighbourhood village of ours.'

'Great job done. By the way, what did he steal?' I asked.

'How can he steal when we are guarding the office madam ji? He was trying to take out the tube lights of the office signboard outside.'

'Oh, it's only that, poor fellow', I thought and said, 'Still a good job done. Other bigger thieves will not venture this way.'

'Madam ji, one more thing. Afterwards we found that two tube lights, which were not working earlier, are now working beautifully.' Madanji concluded his report.

The incident was of huge importance to Madan ji within his context of work. But, for madam, the importance level was not that high as her work context is much bigger. But, what is important for the person with 'greater area' is that, he/she must allow the fluid to flow like the law in science in terms of listening with attention, small appreciation, patting at the back. Then the person at 'smaller area' will become more motivated to increase his flow-rate further.

Concept of Work

Work (as per Physics) is said to be done if force applied on an object results in displacement of the object. But, there is a catch. If the displacement is in the direction of force, it is called positive work. Like, you are pushing an object from left to right and the object also moves from left to right. This is positive work. There is a reverse situation where the displacement takes place in the opposite direction w.r.t force. A typical example is friction. It just opposes the motion – if the object wants to move to the right, friction wants it to move to the left and vice versa.

Then, there is a third case, where the force and displacements are perpendicular. In such cases, work done is scientifically zero. Like one is holding a bag on his shoulder and moving in some direction. The force of gravity is pulling the bag downward and the movement is perpendicular. So, gravity is not doing any work in such case.

☞ In life situation, there are typically two kinds of people – optimists and pessimists. An optimist always puts effort in the desired direction and sees the best of the world, while a pessimist puts effort and sees the opposite. An optimist finds the positive in the negative, but the pessimist can only find the negative even in the positive.

☞ The optimists build strong conviction, accept responsibility, lead to better relationships, are self-motivated & ambitious. On the other hand, the pessimists are generally gossipmongers, are of critical nature, avoid taking responsibility, spoil the relationship, are close-minded, are in justifying mode and so on. Our aim should be to understand ourselves and try to get into the mode of optimism as much as possible as that only will make the progress in the positive desired direction and will make the life meaningful.

☞ In terms of the two circles of life we mentioned taking reference of first habit, the optimists continuously work on the circle of influence and tries to expand it as far as possible. This results in positive work – displacement in the desired direction. On the other side, the pessimists get bogged down in the circle of concern, weakening the circle of influence. This results in negative work – displacement in undesired direction.

☞ And, there is a third kind, the perpendicular type, who has neither positive nor negative perceptions. They are also non-contributors.

Let's read a story regarding positivity and negativity:

Story of bird dog

An avid duck hunter was in the market for a new bird dog. His search ended when he found a dog that could actually walk on water to retrieve a hunted duck. Shocked by his find, he was sure none of his friends would believe him. He decided to break the news to a friend of his, a pessimist by nature, by inviting him to hunt with him with his new dog.

As they waited by the shore, a flock of ducks flew by. They fired and a duck fell into the water. The dog responded and jumped into the water to retrieve it. The dog, however, did not sink, but instead walked across the water to retrieve the bird, never getting more than his paws wet. This continued all day long; each time a duck fell, the dog walked across the surface of the water to retrieve it.

The pessimist watched carefully, saw everything, but never so much ventured a single word. On the drive home, the hunter now asked his friend, 'Did you notice anything unusual about my new dog?'

'I sure did', responded the pessimist, 'he can't swim.'

> ***Some people will always remain negative, whatever happens. And some people will always remain positive, whatever happens. We must learn to ensure that the displacement takes place along the direction of force, resulting in positive work.***

❑❑❑

5. Heat

Heat is a form of energy which gives rise to hotness in an object. It has a direct effect on temperature and change of state. Heat flows from hotter body to colder body to achieve thermal equilibrium. Heat causes molecular movement in the solid, liquid and vapours. The subject Thermodynamics is based on heat and work. We will try to draw equivalence to some of the concepts.

Effect of Heat on Temperature

Heat is closely related to temperature. **The mathematical equation is: Q = m x C x t; where Q is the heat energy supplied, m is the mass of the object, C is the specific heat and t is the change of temperature.** With supply of heat, temperature of a body will increase and with withdrawal of heat, temperature will decrease. For the same mass of object of same material, more the heat supplied, more will be the increase in temperature. For the same mass of two objects of different materials, the change of temperature will depend on a factor called specific heat. More the specific heat less will be the increase of temperature for the same heat input.

Now, what is specific heat? It is the quantity of heat required to increase the temperature of 1 kg of a particular material by 1 degree C. It is a property of material. To have a feel of it, following are the values of specific heats of some of the common materials (in kJ/ Kg K):

Water	4.187	Ice (0° C)	2.09	Ice (-40° C)	1.8		
Iron	0.46	Lead	0.13	Mercury	0.14	Alumin-ium	0.87
Paper	1.34	Rubber	2.01	Brick	0.9	Graphite	0.7

It is clearly visible from the table that (i) specific heats are different for different materials, (ii) water has a very high value (implying that lot of heat is required to increase the temperature of water), (iii) it is very easy to raise the temperature of materials with low specific heats like lead, mercury.

- ☞ What is the equivalence in life? Everyday during our conscious life, we interact with situations having different energy levels. In some cases, heat energy is added to the system which increases the temperature of temperament and in some cases heat is extracted, giving rise to loss of temperature. But the extent of rise or fall of temperature for similar kind of situation will depend on individual capability which can be equated to specific heat in Physics (assuming that the property related to mass is equivalent to the social background and will be same for people in similar context) and hence will be different for different people.

- ☞ This can also be equated to our response to opportunities. First of all, the opportunity has to be spotted in life. It never comes saying that, 'Hello, see, I've come, take me'. So, the right source of heat has to be identified first. Now, assuming the potential and competency being same for two individuals, getting benefited from the same opportunity will not be same for two individuals. One may flourish, other may not. One may rise high, other may not be able to scale that height.

☞ That means, the rise in temperature will depend on some individual factor which is equivalent to specific heat. Specific heat here would mean resistance to self-motivation, urge to progress, fire for passion and so on. So, to benefit maximum from a given opportunity, one has to be self-driven, focussed, fired from inside, ready-to-go-attitude, have risk-taking-capability. Otherwise be happy moving in small steps or not moving at all and criticising others.

☞ *There is no elevator to success. You have to take the stairs*

Concept of Latent Heat & Cooling

We have already seen that when heat is supplied to a substance, its temperature increases depending on its mass and specific heat. Its molecular movement and inter-molecular gaps go on increasing and after a certain limit, the state of the substance starts changing at a constant temperature. That means, if we go on heating a piece of ice at -20° C, its temperature will go on increasing till 0° C and then it will start melting (change of state from solid to liquid). The temperature will remain constant till the ice gets completely changed into water at 0°C.

The question rises, what happens to the heat supplied during this time. Why doesn't the temperature rise? Actually, the heat supplied during this period gets utilised in changing the state of the substance from solid to liquid and it is called latent heat of melting (since this heat is not apparently visible).

If we keep on heating that water at 0°C, its temperature will start increasing till it reaches 100°C and then it will start changing to steam (gaseous or vapour state) at that temperature. So again some considerable amount of heat is utilised for this change of state which remains hidden and is called latent heat of vaporisation.

There is a similar phenomenon wherein we observe change of state of water from small open containers at home or the huge oceans to its vapour state much below its boiling point. This is called evaporation. Here also, same latent heat is required for the change of state which the water acquires from the container or the surroundings. As a result, the container or the surrounding becomes cooler and the water acquires higher energy level as water vapour. This concept is used in water cooler, getting cooled under ceiling fan etc etc.

- ☞ In our lives also, there are people who are like this water in desert-cooler or container. They easily acquire higher energy level by absorbing heat for the sake of others and the surrounding gets cooler. They are like Lord Shiva, who gulps the entire poison of the creation and keeps it at his throat (Neelkanth) so that the world has only Amrit.

- ☞ The mentality of these people are far above normal thinking of narrow-minded people whose whole emphasis is only on having and taking more and more. These nobles only know how to give and hence become more rather than having more.

- ☞ These nobles make a positive dent in the society for the benefit of current and future generations. We remember Raja Rammohan Roy, Pandit Ishwarchandra Vidyasagar, Derogio, Dayand Saraswati and the likes for their selfless contribution to social reforms.

- ☞ And, since the heat acquired does not change the temperature for such liquid significantly, their contribution remains silent and hidden for most of the times. But, history is impartial. Hence the bravehearts like Socrates, Galelio and all, who were not appreciated in their times, have become immortals in the journey of history.

- ☞ This can be seen as a further basic concept. Everything in the nature – the sun, the moon, the trees, the butterflies, the honey-bees are doing their duties day in and day out. The sun rises and sets, the flowers in the trees blossom – we take them for granted. They do not ask for any motivation, any recognition. They are doing their duties – the *svadharma,* the law of being. Human being is the only funny exception who needs motivation for doing *svadharma* – a student needs motivation to undertake his basic duty of studying, an employee needs motivation to his organizational duties (for which he is paid as per accepted terms), a citizen needs traffic police to obey traffic rules and so on. The water evaporates at a temperature below boiling point and makes its surrounding cool – just to do its natural duty. When shall we learn or rather when shall we unlearn what we have done to us through so-called modern thoughts?

Lets go through the following story:

The old phone

When I was quite young, my father had one of the first telephones in our neighbourhood. I remember the polished, old case fastened to the wall. The shiny receiver hung on the side of the box. I was too little to reach the telephone, but used to listen with fascination when my mother talked to it. Then I discovered that somewhere inside the wonderful device lived an amazing person. Her name was "Information Please" and there was nothing she did not know. 'Information please' could supply anyone's number and the correct time.

My personal experience with the genie-in-a-bottle came one day while my mother was visiting a neighbour. Amusing myself at the tool bench in the basement, I whacked my finger with a hammer, the pain was terrible, but there seemed no point in crying because there was no one home to give sympathy. I walked around the house sucking my throbbing finger, finally arriving at the stairway. The telephone! Quickly, I ran for the footstool in the parlor and dragged it to the landing climbing up, I unhooked the receiver in the parlor and held it to my ear. "Information, please" I said into the mouthpiece just above my head.

A click or two and a small clear voice spoke into my ear, "Information." "I hurt my finger..." I wailed into the phone, the tears came readily enough now that I had an audience.

"Isn't your mother home?" came the question. "Nobody's home but me," I blubbered.

"Are you bleeding?" the voice asked. "No," I replied. "I hit my finger with the hammer and it hurts."

"Can you open the icebox?" she asked. I said I could.

"Then chip off a little bit of ice and hold it to your finger," said the voice. After that, I called "Information Please" for everything. I asked her for help with my geography, and she told me where Philadelphia was. She helped me with my math. She told me my pet chipmunk that I had caught in the park just the day before, would eat fruit and nuts.

Then, there was the time Petey, our pet canary, died. I called, 'Information Please,' and told her the sad story. She listened, and then said things grown-ups say to soothe a child. But I was not consoled. I asked her, "Why is it that birds should sing so beautifully and bring joy to all families, only to end up as a heap of feathers on the bottom of a cage?"

She must have sensed my deep concern, for she said quietly, "Wayne, always remember that there are other worlds to sing in." Somehow I felt better.

Another day I was on the telephone, "Information Please."

"Information," said in the now familiar voice. "How do I spell 'fix'?" I asked.

All this took place in a small town in the Pacific Northwest. When I was nine years old, we moved across the country to Boston. I missed my friend very much. "Information Please" belonged in that old wooden box back home and I somehow never thought of trying the shiny new phone that sat on the table in the hall. As I grew into my teens, the memories of those childhood conversations never really left me. Often, in moments of doubt and perplexity I would recall the serene sense of security I had then. I appreciated now how patient, understanding, and kind she was to have spent her time on a little boy.

A few years later, on my way west to college, my plane put down in Seattle. I had about half an hour or so between planes. I spent 15 minutes or so on the phone with my sister, who lived there now. Then, without thinking what I was doing, I dialed my hometown operator and said, "Information Please."

Miraculously, I heard the small, clear voice I knew so well, "Information." I hadn't planned this, but

I heard myself saying, "Could you please tell me how to spell fix?"

There was a long pause. Then came the soft spoken answer, "I guess your finger must have healed by now."

I laughed, "So it's really you," I said. "I wonder if you have any idea how much you meant to me during that time?"

"I wonder," she said, "if you know how much your call meant to me. I never had any children and I used to look forward to your calls."

I told her how often I had thought of her over the years and I asked if I could call her again when I came back to visit my sister.

"Please do", she said. "Just ask for Sally."

Three months later I was back in Seattle. A different voice answered "Information". I asked for Sally.

"Are you a friend?" she said. "Yes, a very old friend," I answered.

"I'm sorry to have to tell you this," she said. "Sally had been working part-time the last few years because she was sick. She died five weeks ago."

Before I could hang up she said, "Wait a minute, did you say your name was Wayne?"

"Yes." I answered. "Well, Sally left a message for you. She wrote it down in case you called. Let me read it to you."

The note said, "Tell him there are other worlds to sing in. He'll know what I mean." I thanked her and hung up. I knew what Sally meant. Never underestimate the impression you may make on others.

> ***Sally has been giving only and finally she's gone to the other world to sing in. We all find such people in our lives sometimes or other, who take away the heat of problems, sufferings, issues from us give the effect of soothing. We also should act like them for others, who need our support – may be at emotional level only.***

❑❑❑

6. Light

In this chapter, we will discuss the laws related to light. Light is the form of energy which allows us to see everything. It travels in a straight line and its speed in vacuum is the ultimate speed of the physical world.

Light follows laws of reflection when it is reflected by a reflecting surface. It follows laws of refraction when it enters into a second medium from one medium. The properties of reflection and refraction are used in mirrors and lens with the formation of two kinds of image – real and virtual. Light has dual nature – particle and wave and there are evidences for both.

Let us examine some of the theories and concepts of light.

Laws of Refraction & Optical Illusion

Refraction is the phenomenon of bending of light when it enters from one medium to another. The degree of bending depends on the relative refractive index, which in turn, depends on the optical densities of the media. Values of refractive indices of some material are as follows:

Air: 1.008, Water: 1.33, Ethyl alcohol: 1.36, Glass: 1.52, Diamond: 2.46.

Without going into much numbers, what it means is that light will bend when it enters water from air and also when it enters glass from air. But, since the refractive index of glass is more than water, the bending of light will be more in case of glass.

☞ Refraction of light results in optical illusion to our eyes. We see anything as light comes from the object to our eyes and the image is formed on our retina and so on. And our eye cannot follow the bending of light, if any. So, if light comes straight from an object to our eyes (which normally happens), we perceive the object at the right place. But, if light comes after bending (because of refraction or reflection), our eyes get deceived and we perceive the object to be towards the last path of the light. This causes optical illusion and results in many physical phenomenon. Mirage is formed in desert, twinkling of stars is perceived by us at night, we see the sun beyond horizon at sunrise and sunset. All these happen due to refraction of light through different layers of air which are at different densities due to different temperature and our eyes follow the last path of light. We also see a straight pencil bent inside water due to refraction of light from water to air.

☞ In our life also, we see situations with our understanding. If light comes straight, there is no problem. But, if there is refraction, we do not perceive the context or the incident correctly. Let us examine in little detail how we perceive things.

☞ There is a more appropriate word for this perception, which is paradigm which has been beautifully explained by Stephen Covey in Seven habits of highly effective people. Paradigm means a model, perception, assumption or frame of reference. It is the way we 'see' the world – in terms of perceiving, understanding, and interpreting. It is like a mental map.

☞ We interpret everything we experience through these mental maps. We seldom question their accuracy as we are usually unaware about the maps. Our attitudes and behaviours grow out of those assumptions and our actions get derived from them. Each of us tends to think we see things as they are. But, this is not the case. We see the world, not as it is, but as we are conditioned to see it – the path of the last part of the light rays.

☞ The more aware we are of our paradigms, and the extent to which we have been influenced by our experience, the more we can take responsibility for those paradigms. We can then examine them, test them against reality, listen to others and be open to their perceptions. Thus, we get a larger picture and a far more objective view (the real position of the object after corrections for refractions). This is called Paradigm shift. Let's understand with one example.

Story of cookies

A young lady was waiting for her flight in the boarding room of a big airport. As she would need to wait many hours, she decided to buy a book to spend her time. She also bought a packet of cookies.

She sat down in an armchair, in the VIP room of the airport, to rest and read in peace. Beside the armchair where the packet of cookies lay, a man sat down in the next seat, opened his magazine and started reading.

When she took out the first cookie, the man took one as well. She felt irritated but said nothing. She just thought: "What a nerve! If I was in the mood I would punch him for daring!"

For each cookie she took, the man took one too. This was infuriating her but she didn't want to cause a scene. When only one cookie remained, she thought: "What would this abusive man do now?"

Then, the man, taking the last cookie, divided it into half, giving her one half. "This is too much," she thought. She was much too angry now! She took her book and her things and stormed to the boarding place.

When she sat down in her seat, she looked into her purse to take her eyeglasses. And to her surprise, her packet of cookies was there. Untouched and unopened!

She felt so ashamed! She realized that she was wrong. She had forgotten that her cookies were kept in her purse.

The man had divided his cookies with her, without feeling anger or bitterness while she had been very angry, thinking that she was dividing her cookies with him. And now there was no chance to explain herself nor to apologize.

All throughout, her perception was wrong – she was having mental illusion as she could not follow the bent path of light.

Let's read another story.

Story of lighthouse (taken from Seven Habits of Highly Effective People)

Two battleships assigned to the training squadron had been at sea on maneuvers in heavy weather for several days. I was serving on the lead battleship and was on watch on the bridge as night fell. The visibility was poor with patchy fog, so the captain remained on the bridge keeping an eye on all activities.

Shortly after dark, the lookout on the wing of the bridge reported, 'Light, bearing on the starboard bow.'

'Is it steady or moving astern?' the captain called out.

Lookout replied, 'Steady, captain,' which meant we were on a dangerous collision course with that ship.

The captain then called to the signalman, 'Signal that ship: We are on a collision course, advise you change your course 20 degrees.'

Back came a signal, 'Advisable for you to change course 20 degrees.'

The captain said, 'Send, I am a captain, change course 20 degrees.'

'I'm a seaman second class,' came the reply. 'You had better change course 20 degrees.'

By that time, the captain was furious. He spat out, 'Send, I'm a battleship. Change course 20 degrees.'

Back came the flashing light, 'I'm a lighthouse.'

We changed course.

Law of Reversibility of Light

One of the important laws of optics is the *law of reversibility,* **which states that if you reverse a light ray and send it back along its path it will exactly reverse its entire path**. This means that light which passes through a focal point and hits a converging lens will exit the lens parallel to the axis (as the parallel rays incident on a converging lens pass through the focus).

If we go little deep into it, we will find that light always travels in best possible path. When it is travelling in one medium, it travels in a straight line. When it gets reflected from a surface separating two media, it follows laws of reflection which ensure that light travels the minimum distance. Similarly, when there is refraction of light, it follows the best path depending on the refractive index of the new medium. Hence, when light ray is reversed, it follows the same path as it is already the best path.

☞ In our life also, we follow the path where we normally see others to move. We feel very safe and secure in following precedents. But, the difference here is that whereas light always knows what the best path is, we rarely know about it as we seldom try to analyse in the given context. Hence, sometimes we get the right path and sometimes we do not as we follow the precedents.

☞ The advantage of using previous same path is that you know the road leads somewhere as others have not come back following that route. The risk elements are also normally low in such cases. But, we really don't know how far others have progressed through those known paths. There may be better ways which were never explored as everyone just followed precedence after someone tried this 'just average' way of doing things.

☞ So, as light judiciously analyses and selects the best path at every juncture of its path (be it refraction or reflection), we also should examine the possibilities at every milestone and try to move in the best path or the most optimum path.

Let's read an experiment done with monkeys, which is equally applicable to us:

The monkey experiment

A group of scientists placed five monkeys in a cage where there was a ladder in the middle and a bunch of bananas on top of it. Naturally the monkeys were tempted by their favourite food and they tried to climb the ladder to get the bananas. As soon as any monkey tried that, the others were drenched with cold water. This happened a few times after which whenever a monkey attempted to climb the ladder, the other four would beat it up to restrain it from climbing the ladder. Naturally, the punishment of pouring cold water also stopped and none of them ventured to climb the ladder in spite of the temptation.

The scientists then decided to substitute one of the monkeys. The first thing the new monkey did was to move towards the ladder in an attempt to climb towards the bananas. Immediately, the other monkeys beat him up. After several beatings, the new monkey learned not to climb the ladder even though he never knew why.

Then the second monkey was substituted and the same thing happened. The first substitute monkey also participated in the beating activity. Slowly the third, fourth and fifth monkeys were substituted and the same thing kept on happening.

What was left was a group of five monkeys that though never received cold water treatment, continued to beat up any monkey who attempted to climb the ladder. If it was possible to ask those monkeys why they would beat up all those who attempted to go up the ladder, the most probable answer would be, 'I don't know, that's how things are done around here.'

We are normally tuned to follow the path where we see others moving in front of us. In most of the cases we do not question whether this path is the right one or not. Light energy follows the path which is the best and hence traces it back also when conditions are reversed. But we blindly follow the precedents most of the times and many a times they are found to be irrelevant.

Concept of Power and Focus of Lens

Lens is a close curved surface normally made of glass. It is primarily of two types – convex and concave. The convex lens is bulging out at the centre and thinner at the edges while the concave lens is just opposite. Light rays, when incident on a lens, get refracted into it (air to glass) from one edge and then get refracted out of it from another edge (glass to air) on other side. On account of laws of refraction and the special geometrical shapes of the two edges of the lens, the final emergent rays behave in a special manner if incident rays are parallel.

For a convex lens, the parallel incident rays converge after emerging out from the other side and meet at a point on the principal axis (the imaginary line of symmetry). This point is called the focus and its distance from optical centre of the lens is called focal length (denoted f). Since the focus for convex lens is always on the opposite side of the light source, it is taken as positive.

On the other side for concave lens, the parallel incident rays on one edge, become divergent after emerging from the other edge and they never meet. The emergent rays appear to diverge from a point on the principal axis, on the same side as the light source. This imaginary point is also called focus and its distance from optical centre is called focal length.

Since the focus is always on the same side as the light source, it is taken as negative.

Now, there is another concept called power of lens (denoted as P). **Power of lens is defined as inverse of focal length (measured in m).** So, the power of convex lens is positive and the power of concave lens is negative. Moreover, lesser the value of f, more is the value of P. It means, the convex lens with more power will be able to converge the parallel incident rays nearer to itself compared to the one having less power. Same applies to concave lens (only it indicates the power to diverge).

- ☞ In life also, there are primarily two kinds of people. The people with positive frame of mind, act like convex lens and converge their energy to a focus. Even if the input level is low, due to focussed effort, they are able to generate significant output. Such people are very clear about their circle of influence and they keep concentrating on that only.
- ☞ The other kind of people actually focuses in the virtual direction. So, even if the input energy level is high, due to their pessimistic attitude and lack of commitment, they scatter away the energy in diverse direction. These kinds of people remain engulfed in the circle of

concern (which is beyond one's power of influence) and hence rarely succeed.

☞ Moreover, lesser the focal length, more is the power to the person. It means, the people who can keep their focus very near to their centre of activities, have more power to become successful. Those people, with lack of concentration and perseverance, always have focus far away from their centre of activities and hence always remain confused and incomplete.

Let's go through a story:

We are all motivated either positively or negatively.

When I was in Toronto, I heard a story of two brothers. One was a drug addict and a drunk who frequently beat up his family. The other one was a very successful businessman who was respected in society and had a wonderful family. Some people wanted to find out why two brothers from the same parents, brought up in the same environment, could be so different.

The first one was asked, "How come you do what you do? You are a drug addict, a drunk, and you beat your family. What motivates you?"

He said, "My father." They asked, "What about your father?"

The reply was, "My father was a drug addict, a drunk and he beat his family. What do you expect me to be? That is what I am."

They went to the brother who was doing everything right and asked him the same question. "How come you are doing everything right? What is your source of motivation?"

And guess what he said? "My father. When I was a little boy, I used to see my dad drunk and doing all the wrong things. I made up my mind that that is not what I wanted to be."

Both were deriving their strength and motivation from the same source, but one was using it positively and the other negatively.

Negative motivation brings the desire to take the easier way which ends up being the tougher way.

We are not born as convex or concave lens with defined focal lengths. We acquire the characteristics over a period of time through our upbringing and selection of choices. But, again, they are not final for life. One can change the focal length by adjusting the thickness of the lens. Moreover, if one wants to become positively focussed convex lens from a concave lens, it is possible by thinning the edges. So, it's all in the mind – one has to work consciously.

❑❑❑

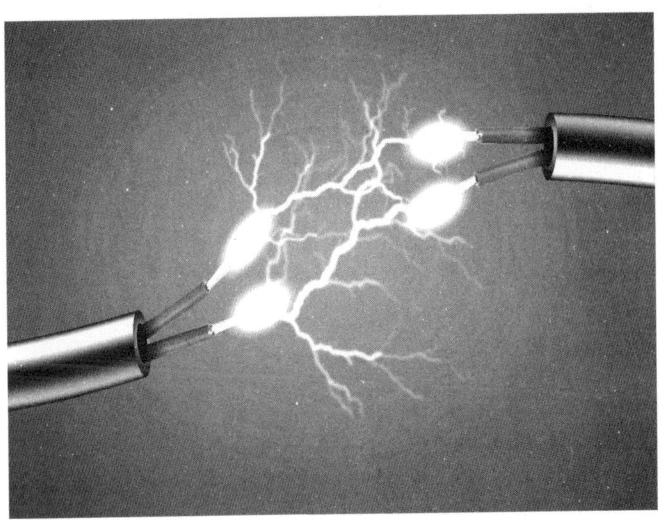

7. Electricity and Magnetism

In electricity, there are two kinds of charges – positive and negative. The negative charge is due to excess of electrons or just the electrons and the positive charge is due to absence of electron/s. The positive and negative charges attract each other and same charges repel each other by a force which is directly proportional to the product of charges and inversely proportional to the square of the distance between them (very similar to law of gravitation). When charges decide to move through a conductor, it results in current (called I). Voltage (or potential difference, called V) is the driver of the current, like the level difference of water is the driver of flow of water.

There are relationships between V and I through Ohm's law; and there are concepts of series and parallel connections & their formulae; heat produced by current flowing through a conductor and so on. Ohm's law gives the definition of resistance and subsequently it is quantified with resistivity, length, area of cross-section etc.

In magnetism, there are two poles – north and south. Their attraction and repulsion are similar to electrical charges. There is close linkage between electricity and magnetism. A current carrying conductor produces magnetic field. Similarly, a moving coil in a magnetic field produces electricity. There are practical applications of these theories in the concepts of motor and generator.

Let us examine some of these theories.

Ohm's Law

This is very fundamental law of electricity. **Ohm's law states that in an electrical circuit, current is proportional to voltage applied. It is expressed as: V = I * R, where R stands for the resistance of the circuit.** So, the other interpretation is that for same voltage available, lesser the resistance, more current can be drawn. Also, for higher R, to sustain the same I, more V is to be applied.

- ☞ In our life there can be similar interpretation. Voltage can be taken as the resource available or the ground reality available to an individual and current can be taken as the energy or enthusiasm with which he faces the reality or the situation. The level of enthusiasm depends purely on the mental resistance as that is the only thing under our control.

- ☞ With reduced mental resistance, in the same situation, different individuals perform to the different degree of success or failure.
- ☞ And the fortunate or unfortunate part is that we are not born with some resistance value. This is acquired through our experience and behaviour system. So, it can always be consciously improved upon. Hence, the game is actually never lost.

One has to know how to live a life. Somebody said:

Dance, as though no one is watching you
Love, as though you have never been hurt before
Sing, as though no one can hear you
Live, as though heaven is on earth

Let's read a story:

A hair raising story

There once was a woman who woke up one morning, looked in the mirror, and noticed she had only three hair on her head.

"Well," she said, "I think I'll braid my hair today?"

So she did and she had a wonderful day.

The next day she woke up, looked in the mirror and saw that she had only two hair on her head.

"H-M-M," she said, "I think I'll part my hair down the middle today?"

So she did and she had a grand day.

The next day she woke up, looked in the mirror and noticed that she had only one hair on her head.

"Well," she said, "today I'm going to wear my hair in a pony tail."

So she did and she had a fun, fun day.

The next day she woke up, looked in the mirror and noticed that there wasn't a single hair on her head.

"YEA!" she exclaimed, "I don't have to fix my hair today!"

How we look at anything in our lives makes the difference between happiness and discontent. So let's make the most of what we have by minimizing the mental resistance.

Law of Series & Parallel Resistance

If two or more resistances are joined in series, the total resistance of the circuit becomes algebraic sum of them: R = R1 + R2 + R3. It also means that in series connection of resistances, current remains same through all of them, whereas voltage gets divided.

If two or more resistances are connected in parallel, the resultant resistance gets reduced by inverse sum law: 1/R = 1/R1 + 1/R2 + 1/R3. It also means that in parallel connection of resistances, voltage remains same for all members whereas current gets divided.

- ☞ In real life, there can be many similarities with these laws. First simile can be if all activities are done in series, the outcome will be least effective with more resistance in path; whereas if activities can be done in parallel, the output can be more effective and attained faster with less resistance.
- ☞ Second simile can be that in series connection, if one element is bad, the current stops in whole circuit. That is the scenario in the non-cohesive groups which are just collection of individuals who hold their individual interests more important in comparison to team interest. In parallel connection, one odd malfunction does not

affect the other elements. The cohesive teams which work keeping individual interests as denominator, succeed much more than others. Even if one odd member is not effective, the team functions as a whole unit and plays to everyone's strength. In a champion cricket team, if the top order batting fails, the middle and even the lower order batsmen deliver results. If one or two star bowlers fail, some other change bowler succeeds or some superlative run-outs take place.

☞ The journey of life consists of all kinds of experiences – high and low. We should add up the high ones following the law of series resistance so that they always remain significant, big and encourage us to move forward. On the other side, we should add up the low ones, the sorrows, following the law of parallel resistance, so that they can never accumulate and we get the strength to overcome them.

God's Boxes

I have in my hands two boxes,
Which God gave me to hold.
He said, "Put all your sorrows in the black box,
And all your joys in the gold."

I heeded His words, and in the two boxes,
Both my joys and sorrows I stored,
But though the gold became heavier each day,
The black was as light as before.

With curiosity, I opened the black,
I wanted to find out why,
And I saw, in the base of the box, a hole,
Which my sorrows had fallen out by.

I showed the hole to God, and mused,
"I wonder where my sorrows could be!"
He smiled a gentle smile and said,
"My child, they're all here with me."

I asked God, why He gave me the boxes,
Why the gold and the black with the hole?
"My child, the gold is for you to count your blessings,
The black is for you to let go."

☞ The next one can be in relationships, if one adds on the petty issues serially, it becomes big and it does not help anyone. It becomes a major resistance in the relationship equation. On the other side, if they are added in inverse sum law, the sum becomes negligible and life becomes much sweeter and prettier. There is a lovely logic for a beautiful Life:

Never try to maintain relations in your life
Just try to maintain life in your relations

Let's read a story:

Build a bridge

Once upon a time, two brothers who lived on adjoining farms fell into conflict. It was the first serious rift in 40 years of farming side by side, sharing machinery, and trading labour and goods as needed without a hitch. Then the long collaboration fell apart. It began with a small misunderstanding and it grew into a major difference, and finally it exploded into an exchange of bitter words followed by weeks of silence.

One morning, there was a knock on John's door. He opened it to find a man with a carpenter's toolbox. 'I'm looking for a few days' work,' he said. 'Perhaps you would have a few small jobs here and there I could help with? Could I help you?'

'Yes', said the older brother. 'I do have a job for you. Look across the creek at that farm. That's my neighbour, in fact, my younger brother. Last week there was a meadow between us and he took his bulldozer to the river levee and now there is a creek between us. Well, he may have done this to spite me, but I'll go him one better. See that pile of lumber by the barn? I want you

to build me an 8 feet fence so that I won't need to see his face anymore.'

The carpenter said, 'I think I understand the situation. I'll be able to do the job that pleases you.' The older brother had to go to town. So, he helped the carpenter to get the materials ready and then he was off for the day. The carpenter worked hard all day measuring, sawing, nailing. About sunset when the farmer returned, the carpenter had just finished his job. The farmer's eye opened wide, his jaw dropped. There was no fence there at all. It was a bridge – a bridge stretching from one side of the creek to the other! A fine piece of work handrails and all – and the neighbour, his younger brother, was coming across, his hand outstretched.

'You are quite a fellow to build this bridge after all I've said and done.' The two brothers stood at each end of the bridge, and then they met in the middle, taking each other's hand. They turned to see the carpenter hoist his toolbox on his shoulder.

'No, wait! Stay a few days. I've a lot of other projects for you,' said the elder brother.

'I'd love to stay on,' the carpenter said, 'but I have many more bridges to build.'

The carpenter knew how to add the resistances in parallel. The world is still liveable because of few people like him.

Effect of Magnetism & Electric Current

Electricity and magnetism are closely linked to each other. When a current-carrying conductor is placed over a compass, the magnetic needle gets deflected. Extrapolating this concept, **when a rectangular coil is placed in a magnetic field and current is passed through it, a force acts on the coil which rotates it continuously. This principle is used in electric motor.** The direction of rotation is given by Fleming's left hand rule (Hold the forefinger, the centre finger and the thumb of your left hand at right angles to each other so that the forefinger points in the direction of magnetic field, centre finger points in the direction of current. Then the direction of thumb points towards the direction of force acting on the conductor).

So, the coil gets the luxury of motion as current flows through it. But, it also knows that the horse-shoe magnet sitting quietly around him is providing the perpendicular magnetic field, without which the electricity cannot impart motion in him.

- ☞ In our lives also, many a times we get success or overcome difficult situations. We put our efforts of current to get those results but, that is not the only input to the process. Most of the times, there are other persons also sitting invisibly and supporting us in our efforts through their whole-hearted physical or mental support or the blessings & best wishes. It is our sincere duty to acknowledge our gratitude to such friends or relatives or mentors or just simple well-wishers who provide the magnetic field for our journey of success.

☞ In fact, as per Hindu philosophy, we are always under debts of five big groups – debt to the God and different gods & goddesses (*Deva-rina)*; debt to historical great men who have given us heavenly teachings of life *(Rishi-rina)*; debt to parents and ancestors *(Pitri-rina);* debt to humanity at large *(Nri-rina)*; and debt to flora and fauna (nature) (*Bhuta-rina)*.We must discharge these debts, to the extent possible, through prayer/ surrender; self-study/practice; serving/ seeking forgiveness; charity and conservation of nature.

☞ We also should learn to act like those great people when situation demands for some of our friends or relatives or even some passers-by so that others also can reach their goals.

We will share a story:

Prayer

A voyaging ship was wrecked during a storm at sea and only two of the men on it were able to swim to a small desert like island. The two survivors, not knowing what else to do, agreed that they had no other recourse but to pray to God. However, to find out whose prayer was more powerful, they agreed to divide the territory between them and stay on opposite sides of the island.

The first thing they prayed for was food. The next morning, the first man saw a fruit-bearing tree on his side of the land and he was able to eat it's fruit. The other man's parcel of land remained barren!

After a week, the first man was lonely and he decided to pray for a wife. The next day, there was a woman who swam to his side of the land. On the other side of the island, again there was nothing!

Soon the first man prayed for a house, clothes, more food. The next day, like magic, all of these were given to him. However, the second man still had nothing!

Finally, the first man prayed for a ship, so that he and his wife could leave the island. In the morning, he found a ship docked at his side of the island. The first man boarded the ship with his wife and decided to leave the second man on the island. He considered the other man unworthy to receive God's blessings, since none of his prayers had been answered.

As the ship was about to leave, the first man heard a voice from heaven booming, "Why are you leaving your companion on the island?"

"My blessings are mine alone, since I was the one who prayed for them," the first man answered. "His prayers were all unanswered and so he does not deserve anything."

"You are mistaken!" the voice rebuked him. "He had only one prayer, which I answered. If not for that, you would not have received any of my blessings."

"Tell me, O God," the first man asked the voice, "What did he pray for that I should owe him anything?"

"He prayed that all your prayers be answered."

For all we know, our blessings are not the fruits of our prayers alone, but those of another praying for us.

> ***My prayer for you today is that all your prayers are answered. Be blessed. "What you do for others is more important than what you do for yourself".***

❑❑❑

Conclusion

We have travelled through few chapters of Physics and tried to find the common threads between the theories of science with our life. This collection is just a sample case of laws and hypothesis where some linkage could be easily established. There may be many more such laws in Physics as well as in other branches of science, which exhibit similar equivalence. But, however exhaustive studies be made, there will be many more hypothesis in life which Science does not cover. The reason is simple– Science covers only physical world – the world of four dimensions (or may be more which are coming up in latest theories) whereas life covers all those physical dimensions plus the human mind, heart, thoughts, emotions, culture and values.

We will presently conclude this thought sharing with a hypothesis which is there in life but not in laws of science.

Law of Miracle

No statement is required for this law. In fact, this law cannot be defined, but it happens, when it is to happen.

A story will explain it better:

Story on Miracle

A little girl went to her bedroom and pulled a glass jelly jar from its hiding place in the closet.

She poured the change out on the floor and counted it carefully. Three times, four times. The total had to be exactly perfect. No chance here for mistakes.

Carefully placing the coins back in the jar and twisting on the cap, she slipped out the back door and made her way 6 blocks to Rexall's Drug Store with the big red Indian Chief sign above the door.

She waited patiently for the pharmacist to give her some attention, but he was too busy at this moment. Tess twisted her feet to make a scuffing noise. Nothing happened. She cleared her throat with the most disgusting sound she could muster. No good. Finally, she took a quarter from her jar and banged it on the glass counter. That did it!

"And what do you want?" the pharmacist asked in an annoyed tone of voice. "I'm talking to my brother from Chicago whom I haven't seen in ages," he said without waiting for a reply to his question.

"Well, I want to talk to you about my brother," Tess answered back in the same annoyed tone. "He's really, really sick...and I want to buy a miracle."

"I beg your pardon?" said the pharmacist.

"His name is Andrew and he has something bad growing inside his head and my Daddy says only a miracle can save him now. So how much does a miracle cost?"

"We don't sell miracles here, little girl. I'm sorry but I can't help you," the pharmacist said, softening a little.

"Listen, I have the money to pay for it. If it isn't enough, I will get the rest. Just tell me how much it costs."

The pharmacist's brother was a well dressed man. He stooped down and asked the little girl, "What kind of a miracle does your brother need?"

"I don't know," Tess replied with her eyes welling up. "I just know he's really sick and Mommy says he needs an operation. But my Daddy can't pay for it, so I want to use my money."

"How much do you have?" asked the man from Chicago.

"One dollar and eleven cents," Tess answered barely audibly.

"And it's all the money I have, but I can get some more if I need to."

"Well, what a coincidence," smiled the man. "A dollar and eleven cents---the exact price of a miracle for little brothers."

He took her money in one hand and with the other hand he grasped her mitten and said "Take me to where you live. I want to see your brother and meet your parents. Let's see if I have the miracle you need."

That well dressed man was Dr. Carlton Armstrong, a surgeon, specializing in neuro-surgery. The operation was completed free of charge and it wasn't long until Andrew was home again and doing well.

Mom and Dad were happily talking about the chain of events that had led them to this place.

"That surgery," her Mom whispered. "was a real miracle. I wonder how much it would have cost?"

Tess smiled. She knew exactly how much a miracle cost...one dollar and eleven cents.... plus the faith of a little child.

> ***In our lives, we never know how many miracles we will need.***
>
> ***A miracle is not the suspension of natural law, but the operation of a higher law.***

MY OATH TO YOU...

When you are sad....I will dry your tears.

When you are scared.....I will comfort your fears.

When you are worried.....I will give you hope.

When you are confused....I will help you cope.

And when you are lost....And can't see the light,
I shall be your beacon.....Shining ever so bright.

This is my oath.....I pledge till the end.

Why you may ask?.....Because you're my friend.

Signed: GOD

Let us rediscover the teachings of our learned ancestors through the writing of Swami Vivekananda:

The bee came to sip the honey, but its feet stuck to the honey-pot and it could not get away. Again and again, we are finding ourselves in that state. Why are we here? We came here to sip the honey, and we find our hands and feet sticking to it. We are caught, though we came to catch. We came to enjoy; we are being enjoyed. We came to rule; we are being ruled. We came to work; we are being worked. We are being worked upon by other minds, and we are always struggling to work on other minds. We want to enjoy the pleasures of life; and they eat into our vitals.

So, there is one main cause of our misery: we are attached, we are being caught. Therefore the Gita says, "Work constantly; work but be not attached; be not caught." Reserve unto yourself the power of detaching yourself from everything, however beloved, however much the soul might yearn for it, however great the pangs of misery you feel if you were going to leave it. The weak has no place here, in this life or any other life. Weakness leads to slavery and all kinds of misery. Strength is life, weakness is death; strength is felicity, life eternal, immortal; weakness is constant strain and misery.

Attachment is the source of all our pleasures now. We are attached to our friends, to our relatives; we are even attached to our intellectual and spiritual works;

we are attached to external objects, so that we get pleasures from them. What again brings misery but this very attachment? We have to detach ourselves to earn joy. The difficulty is that there must be as much power of attachment as that of detachment. It does not mean that you become a wall which can never love and also escapes the miseries of life. The man who never loves, who is hard and stony, escaping most of miseries of life, escapes also from its joys. That is also weakness, that is death. This is also not desirable.

The perfect man can put his whole soul upon that one point of love, yet he is unattached. How comes this? There is another secret to learn.

We are all traders. We are traders in life, we are traders in virtue, we are traders in religion, and we are also traders in love. Trade is a question of buying and selling, giving and taking. There is a good time and there is bad time. We get caught here. How? Not by what we give, but by what we expect. We get misery in return for our love; not from the fact that we love, but from the fact that we want love in return. Desire, want, is the father of all misery.

The great secret of true success, of true happiness, then, is this: the man who asks for no return, the perfectly unselfish man, is the most successful. Ask nothing; want nothing in return. Give what you have to give; it will come back to you – but do not think of that now, it will come back multiplied a thousand-fold – but the attention must not be on that. You are a machine for taking and giving; you take, in order to give. Ask, therefore, nothing in return; but the more you give, the more will come to you. The quicker you can empty the air out of the room, the quicker it will be filled up by the external fresh air. A river is continually emptying itself into the ocean and is continually filling up again.

We shall conclude with the following ultimate analysis:

People are often unreasonable, self-centred:
Forgive them anyway.

If you are honest, people may cheat you, but be honest anyway.

What you spend years to build, someone could destroy overnight.
Build anyway.

The good you do today, people will oftern forget tomorrow.
Do good anyway.

Finally, it is between you and God;
It never was between you and them anyway!!